THE
RESTAURANT
SERVER'S GUIDE
TO
QUALITY CUSTOMER
SERVICE

A Step-by-step Resource
To Increase Your
Success and Income as a
Restaurant Server

William B. Martin

CREDITS
Editor: **Michael Crisp**
Designer: **Carol Harris**
Typesetting: **Interface Studio**
Cover Design: **Carol Harris**
Artwork: **Ralph Mapson**

Copyright © 1986, 1987 by Crisp Publications, Inc.
Printed in the United States of America

Library of Congress Catalog Card Number 85-73177
Martin, William B.
Restaurant Servers Guide to Quality Customer Service
ISBN 0-931961-08-4

PREFACE

In many restaurants the training of newly-hired food and beverage servers is often a catch-as-catch can affair. Limited resources, busy schedules and lack of time prevent restaurant managers from training employees as thoroughly as they would like. This book can help remedy this situation.

This guide is effective at the point of employment because new employees normally want to succeed. THE RESTAURANT SERVER'S GUIDE capitalizes on this situation. The material is also valuable for the continued development of experienced servers. All that is required is a reader, a pencil, a chair, and some time. The book is easily adaptable to either one-on-one or group training situations.

Although the focus of the book is on table service, food servers in other settings, such as cafetarias and institutions, can benefit from the program. Except for a few sections, all exercises and discussion points apply to a wide variety of food service settings.

As you preview THE RESTAURANT SERVER'S GUIDE, you will discover the book promotes active learning through a series of lively applications that not only teach techniques of professional restaurant serving and selling, but also help develop the right attitude toward the job. When the right attitude is combined with proper skills, the result is an outstanding restaurant server. That's exactly what this book delivers.

TO THE MANAGER OR TRAINER

THE RESTAURANT SERVER'S GUIDE is designed to make your job as trainer more effective, and we hope, a bit easier. This program is NOT intended to replace on-the-job training, rather it simply sets the stage for the effective hands-on training that follows.

The program is divided into *three* parts. PART I covers fundamental skills required to be a successful restaurant server. PART II provides optional work sheets which communicate important information to the newly-hired server and PART III focuses on suggestive selling and customer relation skills.

Introduce Parts I and II Right Away.

Parts I and II can be completed by the new employee the first day on the job; or even better BEFORE the first day. The work sheets in Part II can be removed or copied, and handed-out individually.

Wait A Week or Two Before Assigning Part III to New Employees.

Part III requires some knowledge of the menu and a general sense of how the restaurant works. I have found that newly-hired restaurant servers get much more out of Part III after some job experience. Don't wait too long. One or two weeks is about right for most trainees.

Provide Feedback and Discussion.

Your trainees will want to discuss the exercises in the program. Questions may arise that only you can answer. That is why *three* feedback and discussion sessions are suggested. Once the trainee completes each Part, a meeting should be arranged. A discussion or quiz is recommended after Part II covering table numbers, prices and menu abbreviations.

The exercises on TIMELINESS and SAYING THE RIGHT THING in Part I specifically ask for your input and work best when you clearly define your restaurant's service standards.

Feedback and discussion, facilitated by this program, should help you establish a supportive relationship with new employees. The time you devote to these sessions will be well invested.

Best wishes. I hope you find this program to be a valuable training tool.

William B. Martin

William B. Martin

TO THE RESTAURANT SERVER:

In a short while, after completing Part I of this book, you will begin to understand many secrets of professional restaurant serving. What you learn, and the changes you make after completing this program, are far more important than the time it takes to finish. DO NOT READ SO FAST THAT YOU MISS SOMETHING.

If you are new to the job, you will be ready to master Part II within a day or two of completing Part I. Then after a week or so on the job, you will be ready for Part III. Understanding and applying what you learn in *each* part is key to your success as a restaurant server.

Being a restaurant server should be fun and challenging. Restaurant serving is a profession with many principles, methods and skills which need to be learned. Therefore, the way to make the most of your restaurant serving career is to enjoy it fully, but also learn all you can about the process. It is the combination of your attitude and skills that will help you develop into a professional restaurant server.

Good Luck!

William B. Martin

William B. Martin

P.S. The person who provided this program wants you to keep it for future reference. If you have a problem as you work through this book, ask your supervisor for help.

CONTENTS

PART I

In the next sixty pages, you will understand THE FUNDAMENTALS for succeeding as a RESTAURANT SERVER.

MAKE YOUR CHOICE NOW

SERVER SUCCESSES	**SERVER FAILURES**

Those who genuinely enjoy working with and for other people

Those who would rather be working alone or with ''things'' instead of people

Those who can make the customer feel important

Those who need to be the center of attention

Those who have a high energy level and enjoy a fast pace

Those who enjoy working at a leisurely pace

Those who view their job primarily as a salesperson

Those who view their job primarily as a server

Those who are flexible and can adapt to new demands and experiences

Those who like to always do things their way

Those who allow customers to be right (sometimes even when they are not)

Those who must always be right and let others know it

Add your own:

Add your own:

_____

_____

_____

_____

_____

_____

> The difference between a professional and non-professional restaurant server is a matter of sensitivity, sincerity, attitude and selling skills—all of which can be learned.

WHAT YOU KNOW AND WHAT YOU NEED TO LEARN

WHAT DO YOU ALREADY KNOW?	Yes	No
Have you previously been employed as a food server?	☐	☐
Was the operation similar to this one?	☐	☐

	Consider-able	Some	Very Little
How would you describe the training you have received as a food server?	☐	☐	☐

WHAT DO YOU NEED TO LEARN?	Yes	No
Are you generally open to new experiences?	☐	☐
Are you willing to learn new or different ways of doing a job you have previously performed?	☐	☐
Do you believe there are still some things you can learn that will make you a better food server?	☐	☐

(The service skills inventory on the facing page will help you determine what you need to learn).

Linda was an experienced food server. She worked three years in an upscale dinner house. She thought she knew everything there was to know about food service until she moved to another city and took a job waiting tables in a very busy family diner. Linda soon discovered she had many new things to learn. Realizing this helped her succeed in her new position.

SERVICE SKILLS INVENTORY

This self-rating scale will help identify those service areas that you may need to learn more about to improve your service skills. Place a check in the appropriate column.

ABILITY TO—	Know nothing. Need to learn all I can.	Know a little. Need to learn more.	Know quite a bit. Need some brushing up.	Know all there is to know.
1. Provide timely service				
2. Be flexible and accommodating to customer needs				
3. Anticipate customer needs in advance				
4. Use effective communication skills				
5. Solicit feedback from customers.				
6. Be well organized getting the job done				
7. Show a positive attitude, even when the going gets tough				
8. Convey positive body language				
9. Tune-in to the special needs of customers				
10. Make helpful suggestions to customers				
11. Use appropriate language at all times				
12. Speak in a friendly, hospitable tone of voice				
13. Be an effective sales person				
14. Handle difficult customers in a gracious, constructive way				

See author's comments on page 68.

It's not enough to just take orders and serve food. You also need the right personality.

Customers want more than simply to be fed. They want to be treated well.

Your customers want to feel
★ comfortable & relaxed
★ safe from harm & disease
★ important and appreciated

In short, they want you to CARE ABOUT THEM!

HOW GOOD ARE YOUR CUSTOMER RELATIONS SKILLS?

Alvin is basically quiet and shy. Even though he is not naturally outgoing, he likes people and enjoys working in a fast-paced environment. Working well with fellow employees and customers can help Alvin bring his customer relations potential to the surface.

CUSTOMER RELATIONS POTENTIAL SCALE

Circle where you fall on each scale.

Left	5	4	3	2	1	Right
I control my moods most of the time.	5	4	3	2	1	I have no control over my moods.
I can be pleasant to people even if they are not nice to me.	5	4	3	2	1	I can't be pleasant to people unless they are nice to me.
I get along well with others.	5	4	3	2	1	I have difficulty getting along with others.
I enjoy helping people.	5	4	3	2	1	Let other people help themselves.
I can apologize for mistakes even if I did not make them.	5	4	3	2	1	I would not apologize for a mistake I didn't make.
I have good command of language and can use it effectively.	5	4	3	2	1	I am insecure about my ability to communicate verbally with others.
I am good at remembering names and faces.	5	4	3	2	1	I can't remember names or faces.
I smile often.	5	4	3	2	1	It is difficult for me to smile.
Pleasing others is satisfying to me.	5	4	3	2	1	I have no desire to please others.
Cleanliness and grooming are important.	5	4	3	2	1	Being well groomed isn't that big a deal.

TOTAL SCORE _____

If you rated yourself 40 or above, you have the potential to be excellent with customers. If you scored between 25 and 40, you may need more confidence in customer relation skills before working with the public. If you rated yourself less than 25, working as a restaurant server is probably a poor choice for you.

WHAT IS QUALITY CUSTOMER SERVICE?

Two primary dimensions make up quality customer service: the *procedural* dimension and the *personal* dimension. Each is critical to the delivery of QUALITY service.

THE PROCEDURAL SIDE of service consists of the established systems and procedures to deliver products and/or service.

THE PERSONAL SIDE of service is how service personnel, (using their attitudes, behaviors and verbal skills) interact with customers.

The exercises and activities in this book reflect both dimensions of QUALITY SERVICE.

QUALITY SERVICE EXERCISE

The diagrams below show the procedural and personal dimensions in graphic form.

The vertical axis represents the degree of procedural service and the horizontal axis reflects a measure of personal service.

Study each diagram below. HOW WOULD YOU DESCRIBE THE NATURE OF THE SERVICE REFLECTED IN EACH DIAGRAM? Indicate your responses in the spaces provided.

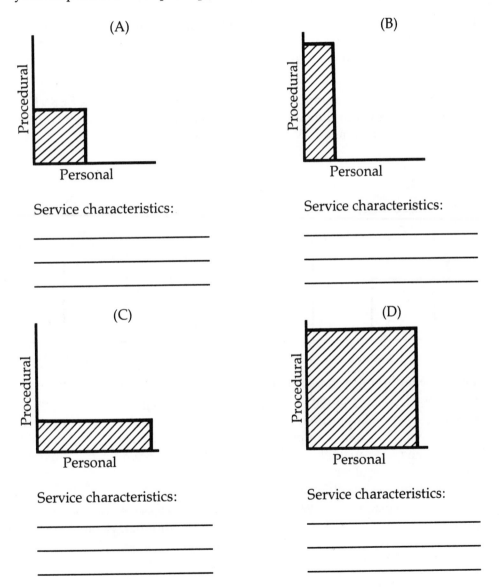

(A)

Service characteristics:

_____
_____
_____

(B)

Service characteristics:

_____
_____
_____

(C)

Service characteristics:

_____
_____
_____

(D)

Service characteristics:

_____
_____
_____

See the author's response to each diagram on the next page.

FOUR TYPES OF SERVICE

Diagram A:
The Freezer

This reflects an operation that is low in both personal and procedural service. This "freezer" approach to service communicates to customers, "We don't care."

Diagram B:
The Factory

This diagram represents proficient procedural service but a weakness in the personal dimension. This "factory" approach to service communicates to customers, "You are a number. We are here to process you."

Diagram C:
The Friendly Zoo

The "friendly zoo" approach to service is very personal but lacks procedural consistency. This type of service communicates to customers, "We are trying hard, but don't really know what we're doing."

Diagram D:
Q.C.S.

This diagram represents QUALITY CUSTOMER SERVICE. It is strong in both the personal and procedural dimensions. It communicates to customers, "We care and we deliver."

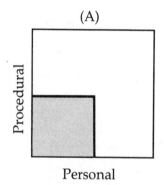

(A)

Procedural / Personal

The "freezer" service characteristics:

Procedural	Personal
slow	insensitive
inconsistent	cold or impersonal
disorganized	apathetic
chaotic	aloof
inconvenient	uninterested

Message to customers: **"We don't care."**

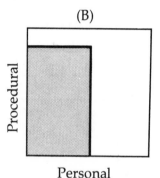

(B)

Procedural / Personal

The "factory" service characteristics:

Procedural	Personal
timely	insensitive
efficient	apathetic
uniform	aloof
	uninterested

Message to customers: **"You are a number. We are here to process you."**

FOUR TYPES OF SERVICE (Continued)

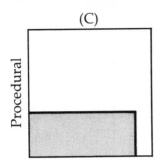

(C)

Procedural | Personal

The "friendly zoo" service characteristics:

Procedural	Personal
slow	friendly
inconsistent	personable
disorganized	interested
chaotic	tactful

Message to customers: **"We are trying hard, but we don't really know what we're doing."**

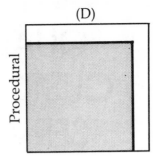

(D)

Procedural | Personal

Quality Customer Service characteristics:

Procedural	Personal
timely	friendly
efficient	personable
uniform	interested
	tactful

Message to customers: **"We care, and we deliver!"**

THREE REASONS WHY *QUALITY CUSTOMER SERVICE* IS IMPORTANT

I. *CUSTOMERS HAVE COME TO EXPECT QUALITY SERVICE*

Today's customers are better educated, more experienced and expect more than they did twenty years ago. Restaurant customers anticipate quality customer service as a matter of course. If they don't receive it, they don't come back.

II. *COMPETITION DEMANDS QUALITY SERVICE*

There are more restaurant choices today than ever before. To survive, most restaurants strive to provide quality food in a clean environment. The primary factor that separates the most successful restaurants from others is SERVICE. Quality customer service provides the competitive edge.

III. *QUALITY SERVICE IS THE KEY TO BUSINESS SUCCESS*

This all boils down to the fact that your restaurant has to EXCEL in service in order to build a strong and loyal customer base. In the final analysis, it is your customer that pays your wages. Without customers there would be no restaurant and no job. Quality customer service is, indeed, the key to business success.

QUALITY CUSTOMER SERVICE

is

important
to my
restaurant

BUT,

WHAT ABOUT ME?

WHY SUCCESS IN CUSTOMER SERVICE IS IMPORTANT TO YOU

Common sense should tell you that your success with customers will increase the amount of money you make (whether in wage increases or tips). It will also make you more promotable. Money aside, success in customer service also provides many PERSONAL benefits.

Read each statement below. Determine *which are true and which are false* about the benefits quality customer service can bring to you.

(Check your answers with those of the author at the bottom of the page.)

True or False

_____ 1. Working with customers is usually more enjoyable than working at a routine technical job.

_____ 2. Improving interpersonal skills can help develop a personality.

_____ 3. The ability to provide the best possible customer service is a continuous challenge that keeps a job interesting.

_____ 4. Most top executives lack effective customer relations skills.

_____ 5. Ongoing success with customers can lead to better job security and opportunity for promotion.

_____ 6. Learning to treat customers as special people has a "carry over" value to future jobs.

_____ 7. What you learn about customer service in an entry level position is often more important than the money you make.

_____ 8. Service jobs where you meet the public are easier than most technical jobs.

_____ 9. Skill in performing the mechanics of your job is more important than your attitude about how you perform it.

_____ 10. Smiles are contagious.

ANSWERS: 1. T 2. T 3. T 4. F (Many top executives acknowledge that effective customer relations skills helped them get to the top.) 5. T 6. T 7. T 8. F (Customer relations jobs are, in fact, more demanding because they require you to stay positive all the time.) 9. F (Your attitude towards the job is at least as important as your job skills.) 10. T

TIME IS OF THE ESSENCE.

A STITCH IN TIME SAVES NINE.

TIME IS MONEY.

Karen earned her waitress stripes by being the most time cons-
cious server in the restaurant. She was always on time to work
and always on time serving her customers. When she needed
to be fast, she was fast, and when the flow required her to slow
down, she could. Adjusting her timeliness to her customer's
needs was one of Karen's secrets to her table service success.

FASTER THAN A SPEEDING BULLET . . .

TIMELINESS

HOW TIMELY SHOULD YOU BE?

Knowing the service time requirements for your operation is critical for quality service.

Six important customer contact points are listed below. Indicate what you think the response time should be for each. Then, ask your supervisor or trainer to do the same.

After you have both responded, discuss the differences with your trainer or supervisor to learn more about the timing needs of your job.

CUSTOMER CONTACT POINT:	YOUR RESPONSE	MANAGER'S/ TRAINER'S RESPONSE
1. A customer walks in the door. He/She should be greeted within _____ minutes.	_____	_____
2. A party is seated at a table. They should be greeted within _____ minutes.	_____	_____
3. A customer orders a beverage. He/She should receive it within _____ minutes after placing the order.	_____	_____
4. A party of three order meals. They should be served within _____ minutes of placing the order.	_____	_____
5. The customer wants nothing more to eat or drink. The check should be at the table within _____ minutes.	_____	_____
6. The customer has paid and is waiting for change or a credit card receipt. This should be completed within _____ minutes.	_____	_____

See author's comments on page 68.

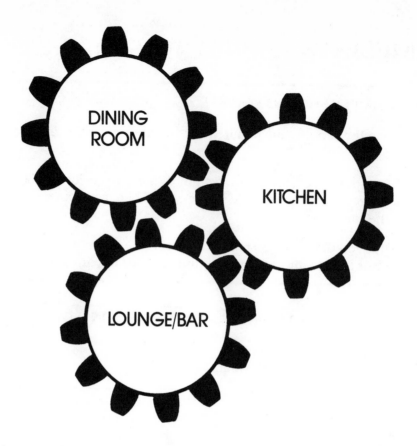

No one part of a restaurant is separate from the other parts. The activities and outcomes of one part affect the operation of ALL THE PARTS.

A well-run restaurant works like the gears of a fine clock. Each part does its share to contribute to the whole. Like a clock, all the gears must mesh smoothly together, or the system will break down.

EACH PART OF THE RESTAURANT DEPENDS ON THE OTHER TO RUN SMOOTHLY AND MAINTAIN A . . .

STEADY FLOW OF SERVICE

FLOW OF SERVICE EXERCISE

As a server, your job is to help provide **a steady flow of service.**

Service at its best, is organized into small increments, or steps. These steps should then proceed in a smooth steady manner.

A steady flow produces timely service. A breakdown in the flow produces slow or inconsistent service.

As a server, you must—

1. Establish a steady flow of service to your customers, and

2. Understand how the other parts of the restaurant depend on you to maintain this flow.

EXERCISE: Read each situation below. Check whether it would tend to cause a breakdown (−) in the flow or insure (+) steady service in the restaurant.

	Would cause flow breakdown (−)	Would enhance the flow (+)
1. Good communication between the service staff and the kitchen	_____	_____
2. A new employee on the job	_____	_____
3. A busperson slow to bus tables after customers leave	_____	_____
4. A fellow server helping out when there is a chance	_____	_____
5. A server who has each table in his/her section at a different place of the meal cycle	_____	_____
6. Arrival of a large group of customers at the same time	_____	_____
7. A server anticipating service needs in advance	_____	_____
8. Shortage of help in the kitchen	_____	_____
9. An inexperienced food server	_____	_____
10. A server who plans his/her steps ahead of time	_____	_____

ANSWERS: 1. + 2. − 3. − 4. + 5. + 6. − 7. + 8. − 9. − 10. +

QUALITY SERVICE REQUIRES . . .
BEING ONE STEP AHEAD
OF
THE CUSTOMER.

Food servers who anticipate well are always one step ahead of their customers. Products and service are provided BEFORE customers have to ask. Timing is adjusted to what will happen next as well as to what just happened. Effective anticipation requires knowing what is going to occur and knowing what customer needs you will have to meet.

Patrick and Ellen are comparing tips one day after their shift. Patrick has made about twice as much as Ellen.

Ellen: "Okay, hotshot, how do you do it?"

Patrick: "No big secret really. I always try to think one step ahead of my customers so they don't have to ask for anything. Anticipate correctly and you can 'wow' them every time."

ANTICIPATE YOUR CUSTOMERS' NEEDS!

Ask: What will my customer need next?

Then: Provide what they will need next, **without requiring them to ask for it.**

Following are ten situations commonly found in restaurants. After each, write what you think the customer will need next:

SITUATION   **ANTICIPATED NEED**

1. A couple orders one dessert   _____

2. A customer with a half cup of coffee   _____

3. A family with two small children   _____

4. You serve a customer a big, gooey, chili-cheeseburger.   _____

5. A couple is celebrating a birthday   _____

6. Two older customers order a single meal   _____

7. A customer finished with his meal is looking around   _____

8. A group of four is informed they have a half-hour wait before being seated in the dining room   _____

9. Businessmen talking and making notes on a napkin   _____

10. Two people who announce they are in a hurry   _____

_____

See author's comments on page 68.

PROVIDING QUALITY SERVICE
REQUIRES YOU TO . . .

COMMUNICATE CLEARLY

Clear communication occurs when the MESSAGE SENT

is the same as the MESSAGE RECEIVED

But, being a successful sender is not always easy.

Being a successful receiver (listener) is even more difficult.

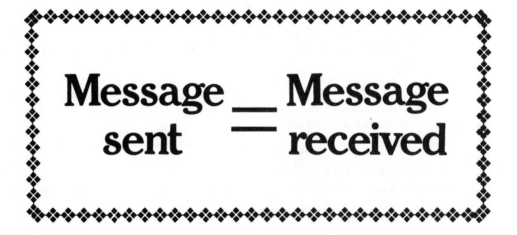

$$\text{Message sent} = \text{Message received}$$

After Ralph takes an order he always repeats it back to the customer. By providing this feedback, he helps guarantee his customers get exactly what they want. Moreover, mistakes are caught before they embarass him, anger the cutomer and cost the restaurant money.

DO YOU KNOW HOW TO COMMUNICATE EFFECTIVELY?

If you do, see if you can identify the **true** statements below.

_____ 1. You should try to impress customers about how knowledgeable you are.

_____ 2. You should always maintain the self-esteem of your customers.

_____ 3. Repeating an order back to a customer can help to eliminate misunderstandings.

_____ 4. Making eye contact with the person to whom you are talking is not very important.

_____ 5. While talking with a customer, you should use words that he/she will understand.

_____ 6. Silence on the part of the customer usually indicates understanding and acceptance of your message.

_____ 7. The more you talk, the better you communicate.

_____ 8. Effective listening skills are developed naturally.

_____ 9. It is important to listen not only to what people say, but also the feelings they are expressing.

_____ 10. When coaching or helping another server, you should focus on that person's performance; not personality.

_____ 11. Your tone of voice communicates as much, or more, of your actual message as the words themselves.

_____ 12. Body language will send direct messages to others.

_____ 13. Misunderstanding a customer's order is really not a serious problem.

_____ 14. Effective communication with customers is always more important than effective communication among fellow employees.

_____ 15. Good servers keep their manager well informed at all times.

Answers: True statements are 2, 3, 5, 9, 10, 11, 12, and 15.

QUALITY SERVICE MEANS . . .

SAYING THE RIGHT THING

A 275 pound man had just finished his dinner at a local steak house when the waiter walked up and said, "Boy, you made that meal disappear fast!" Later, the waiter couldn't understand why the customer complained to the manager.

Knowing the *right thing* to say at the *right time* is an important skill to learn if you are going to be a successful food server. Language that turns guests off must be avoided. The skilled food server is always tactful and aware of just what to say, and how to say it.

SAYING THE RIGHT THING

When talking with customers, you must consider the ACTUAL WORDS to use. WHAT SHOULD YOU SAY TO YOUR CUSTOMERS?

> In the space below, write out a "typical" script that you could use when interacting with your customers. Include a greeting, the words you would say to take an order, and what you would say upon delivering the check.

My greeting would be:_____

_____

_____

_____

I would take the order by saying:_____

_____

_____

_____

When delivering the check, I would say:_____

_____

_____

_____

_____

_____
REVIEW YOUR CHOICE OF WORDS IN THIS EXERCISE WITH YOUR SUPERVISOR OR TRAINER.

AS A SERVER YOU WORK FOR CUSTOMERS AS WELL AS YOUR MANAGER

CUSTOMERS PAY YOUR SALARY!

Therefore, it is important for you to know . . .

What your customers want?
What they need?
What they think?
How they feel?
What suggestions they have?
Whether they are satisfied?

A family-fun restaurant has initiated an aggressive program to solicit customer feedback. A dining room employee is assigned the task of personally asking guests at each table to fill out a feedback card. If the guests agree, the card is left at the table with a pencil. The guests can leave the card in a box at the front of the restaurant upon leaving. According to the restaurant's manager, several important improvements have been made in the operation as a result of customer suggestions. "This program has been invaluable," she states.

CUSTOMER FEEDBACK

Most restaurants have methods to obtain feedback. Several ways to find out what customers are thinking and feeling about the restaurant are listed below. Place a check (✔) by those feedback methods you believe are in use at your establishment.

☐ Listening carefully to what customers have to say.

☐ Checking back during the meal.

☐ Asking customers to fill out feedback cards.

☐ Providing a phone number and name to call for questions, problems or suggestions.

☐ Having the manager stop by the table to ask how things are.

☐ Asking the host/hostess to solicit feedback as customers leave.

☐ Responding constructively to customer complaints.

☐ Noting customers' positive as well as negative comments.

☐ Other: _____

_____

_____

_____

_____

SERVICE, TIPS & BASEBALL

– Being a restaurant server is like playing baseball.

– When you receive a good TIP, you know you have scored.

– Like a ballgame, you can sometimes do everything right and still not win.

– Your TIP BATTING AVERAGE however will increase when you cover the bases correctly.

YOU ARE AT BAT

COVER ALL THE BASES TO EARN A TIP!

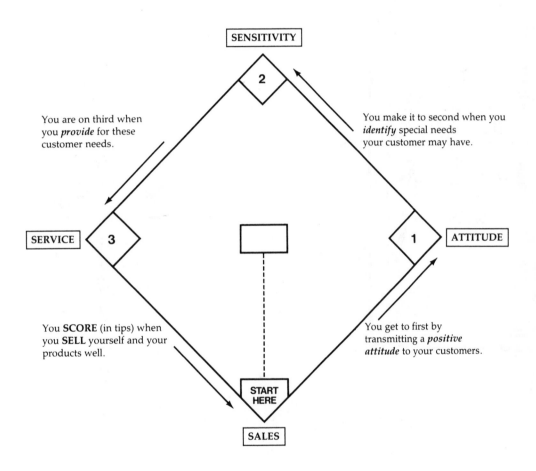

SENSITIVITY

2

You are on third when you *provide* for these customer needs.

You make it to second when you *identify* special needs your customer may have.

SERVICE   3

1   ATTITUDE

You **SCORE** (in tips) when you **SELL** yourself and your products well.

You get to first by transmitting a *positive attitude* to your customers.

START HERE

SALES

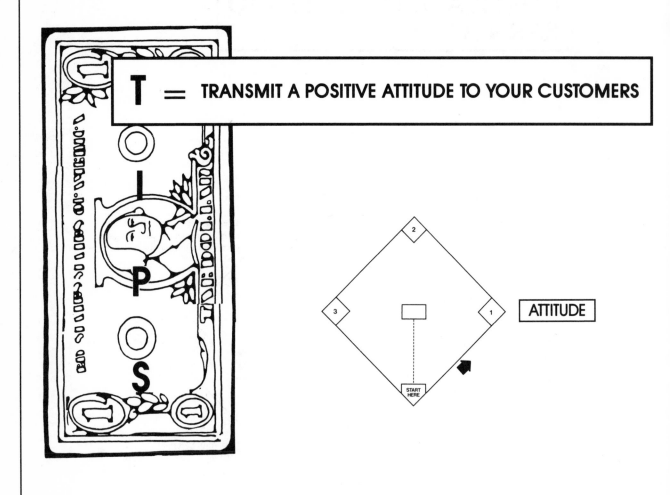

T = **TRANSMIT A POSITIVE ATTITUDE TO YOUR CUSTOMERS**

ATTITUDE

Marge was a likeable person. Her team members at the restaurant where she worked always found her in a good mood. Her customers appreciated her sunny disposition and often requested to sit in her section. When business took a temporary downswing, it came as no surprise that Marge kept working while other waitresses with more seniority were laid off.

MANY SERVERS DO NOT GET TO FIRST BASE...BECAUSE OF ATTITUDE

If you don't get to first base with your customers, the game is over before it begins.

Nothing gets you to first base better than transmitting a **positive attitude** to customers. The **attitude** you project depends on the way you view your job as a restaurant server. To measure your attitude about working as a server, complete this exercise.

CIRCLE THE EXTENT YOU AGREE OR DISAGREE WITH THE STATEMENT.

		Agree		**Disagree**	
1. I am enthusiastic about being a server.	5	4	3	2	1
2. I can approach customers, regardless of age, appearance or behavior with a positive attitude.	5	4	3	2	1
3. On bad days, when nothing goes right, I can still be positive.	5	4	3	2	1
4. I am proud to tell friends I serve in a restaurant.	5	4	3	2	1
5. There is nothing demeaning about being a restaurant server.	5	4	3	2	1
6. Having difficult customers does not cause me to be negative.	5	4	3	2	1
7. The idea of being a professional server challenges me.	5	4	3	2	1
8. Being a restaurant server can be great fun.	5	4	3	2	1
9. I enjoy pleasing others.	5	4	3	2	1
10. Being a good restaurant server is what I really enjoy.	5	4	3	2	1

TOTAL SCORE = [   ]

If you scored above 40, you have an excellent attitude toward being a restaurant server. If you rated yourself between 25 and 40, you may have serious reservations. A rating below 25 indicates another type of job would probably be best for you.

GETTING TO SECOND BASE

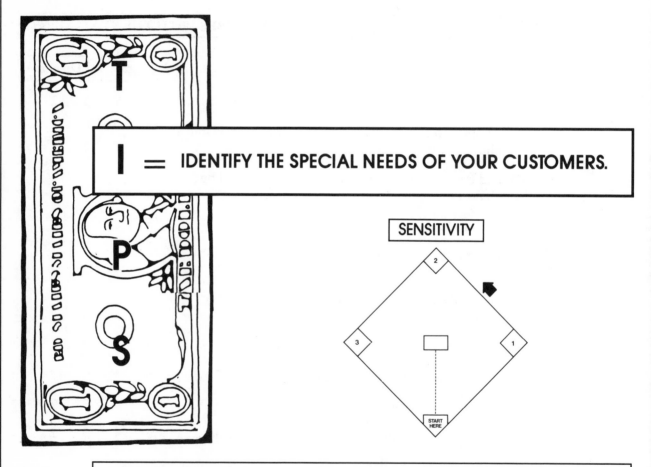

T

I = **IDENTIFY THE SPECIAL NEEDS OF YOUR CUSTOMERS.**

P

S

SENSITIVITY

Jaime is a lead waiter. He is responsible for training all new food servers. Today he wants to introduce the idea of how to identify the special needs of customers to his trainee, but he is not quite sure how to approach the subject. After considerable thought, Jaime decides to act out customer's verbal and nonverbal signals to indicate what their special needs may be. With Jaime giving the cues and the trainee trying to figure them out, today's training session was very successful.

IDENTIFY THE CUSTOMER'S SPECIAL NEEDS

Identifying special needs of each customer requires being sensitive to **both** non-verbal **and** verbal cues. Tuning-in to these messages is called **READING THE CUSTOMER**.

    Reading the customer correctly requires you to pay attention to certain cues. Below are some common ones. Can you think of some special needs that each of these cues may reflect?

CUE:	Potential Special Need

Customer's Age:

    Small children   _____

    Teenagers   _____

    Senior Citizens   _____

Customer's Attire:

    Casual dress   _____

    Business suits   _____

    Formal attire   _____

Group Size and Mix:

    Group of women   _____

    After work bunch   _____

    Large family   _____

Body Language:

    Arms folded   _____

    Looking around   _____

    Looking at watch   _____

Tone of Voice:

    Uptight   _____

    Angry   _____

    Cheerful   _____

See author's comments on page 69.

MAKING THE MOVE TO THIRD BASE

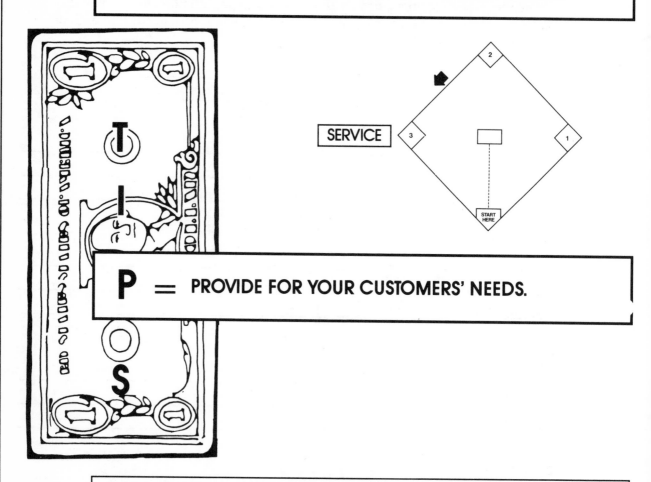

P = **PROVIDE FOR YOUR CUSTOMERS' NEEDS.**

Patrick and Ellen are, once again, comparing tips after their shift. For the first time, Ellen's tips surpass Patrick's.

Patrick: "Great job hotshot. How did you do it?"

Ellen: "Not only have I learned to anticipate, read the guest, and show a positive attitude, I now realize that my customers have psychological and social needs just like me. They like to be liked. They want to feel important. They want to feel good about themselves. I always try to remember that and I think that makes me a better waitress. At least my tips are going up."

FIVE BASIC NEEDS

1. **Need for personal attention**
2. **Need to feel comfortable and relaxed**
3. **Need to belong**
4. **Need to feel important**
5. **Need to be recognized**

WHAT CAN YOU DO TO PROVIDE FOR THESE NEEDS?

Write what you plan to do as a restaurant server to provide for the five basic customer needs.

1. I plan to provide for my customers' need for **personal attention** by: _____

    _____

    _____

2. I plan to provide for my customers' needs to feel **comfortable and relaxed** by: ____

    _____

    _____

3. I plan to provide for my customers' needs to feel they **belong** by: _____

    _____

    _____

4. I expect to provide for my customers' need to feel **important** by: _____

    _____

    _____

5. I will provide for my customers' needs to be **recognized** by: _____

    _____

    _____

See author's comments on page 69.

ROUNDING TO HOME!

PLAY TO WIN!

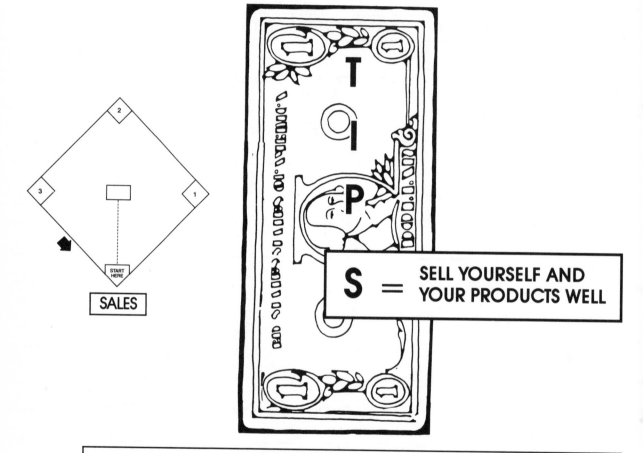

S = **SELL YOURSELF AND YOUR PRODUCTS WELL**

In a training session on selling skills, Jim spoke up, "I don't like to think of myself as a salesperson. Salespeople are pushy and obnoxious. I don't want to be like that."

His trainer responded, "The best salespeople I know are not pushy or obnoxious. They are good listeners who are sensitive to their customer's needs. Selling is a key part of your job as a food server. Like it or not, you have to be an effective salesperson to be a professional food server. If you don't want to sell, maybe this is not the best job for you."

PLAY TO WIN

SELLING YOURSELF

You sell yourself by making a good impression. How well you impress customers depends on:

1. Your physical appearance and personal grooming habits

2. Your body language

3. The tone of your voice

4. Your choice of words

SELLING YOUR PRODUCTS

You sell products by:

1. Expanding your customer's awareness of what is available

2. Mentioning the FEATURES of your products

3. Explaining the BENEFITS of your products

4. Asking for the order

5. Complimenting the customer's choice

HOW GOOD ARE YOU AT THESE TWO FORMS OF SELLING?

☐ I consider myself an expert at both

☐ I need to learn more about one or both

(If you checked the second box, you will be able to find ways to improve your selling skills by completing Parts II and III of this book).

PART I IN REVIEW

I. *Quality service is an integral part of your job – not an extension of it.*

Nothing is more important to your restaurant than customers. Without them, your restaurant could not exist.

II. *Satisfied customers are essential to the success of your business.*

Business grows through satisfied customers. Satisfied customers not only come back, but they also bring their friends.

III. *Quality customer care is learned, not inherited.*

Like mastering any skill, being able to excel in customer care requires practice and experience. The more you put into it, the more you will receive from it.

CASE #1

CASE #1 THE NEW FOOD SERVER

Eric is working as a food server in a family-run restaurant. It is his first experience waiting tables. To help support himself through college, Eric applied at a number of businesses near the school. He had spent the past two summers working as a stockman in a warehouse, and looked for a job that was less physically demanding. When the restaurant called Eric for an interview and then offered him a job, he thought it would be a chance to make some ''easy money.''

Eric's first few weeks on the job were less than successful. The manager called him into the office and said, ''Eric, I think you have the potential to be a good waiter, but so far, you don't seem to be trying very hard. You don't appear to be taking this job very seriously.''

Eric thought for a minute and said ''You're right. I thought it would be a simple job. I didn't realize there would be so much to learn. I thought waiting tables took no skill. I guess this attitude wasn't very good, was it?''

How should the manager respond?

_____

_____

_____

_____

What does Eric need to do to turn the situation around?

_____

_____

_____

_____

Compare your suggestions with the author's on page 69.

PART I
FOLLOW-UP

You have now completed the first half of this program. This is a good time to sit down with your manager and/or trainer to talk about what you have learned. This is also a good time to clarify any questions you may have about the job.

TELL YOUR MANAGER YOU HAVE COMPLETED
THIS SECTION AND ARRANGE A MEETING!

Make notes about what you want to talk about and/or your questions. Also keep a record of any follow-up suggestions or activities once the meeting has been completed.

THINGS TO DISCUSS

1) Questions about our customers.

2) Questions about menu items.

3) Questions about procedures and routines.

4) Some of "my ideas" for improved service.

5) Any follow-up based on this discussion.

PART II

USE THE FOLLOWING PAGES TO
RECORD THE INFORMATION
WHICH WILL HELP YOU LEARN
YOUR JOB QUICKY AND EASILY.

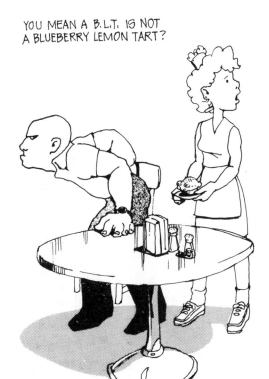

YOU MEAN A B.L.T. IS NOT
A BLUEBERRY LEMON TART?

WORKSHEETS*

*The publisher grants permission for you to
duplicate pages in this section for personal use.

SAMPLE DINING ROOM DIAGRAM

SHOWING TABLE NUMBERS

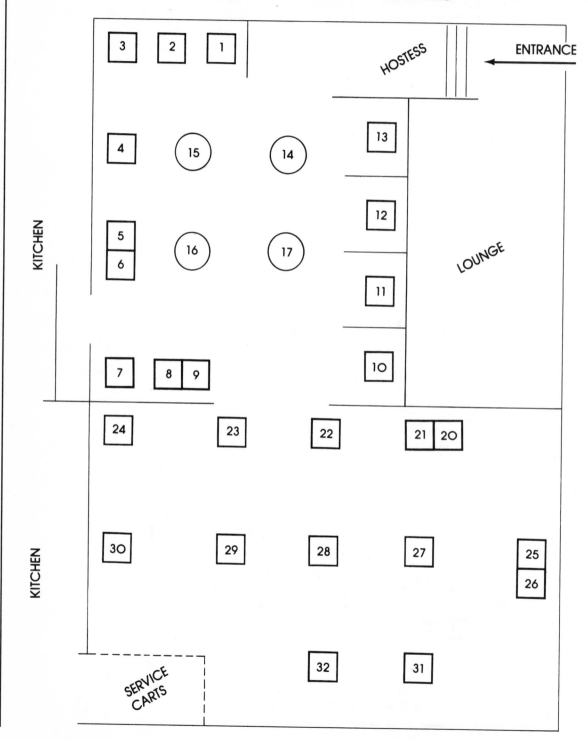

TABLE NUMBER DIAGRAM EXERCISE

Use this page to diagram the dining room and table numbers in your restaurant.

COMMIT THE TABLE NUMBERS TO MEMORY.

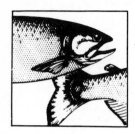

DAILY MENU

ALL MEALS INCLUDE SOURDOUGH BREAD AND BUTTER, AND
FISHERMAN'S RICE.

MESQUITE WOOD CHARCOAL BROILED

```
FRESH PACIFIC RED SNAPPER..................................... 7.95
FRESH FISH BROCHETTE.......................................... 7.95
FRESH IDAHO RAINBOW TROUT..................................... 8.75
FRESH COHO SALMON, PAN SIZED.................................. 9.25
FRESH MAHI MAHI............................................... 9.45
FRESH DELTA CATFISH........................................... 9.55
FRESH MONKFISH................................................ 9.95
FRESH ORANGE ROUGHY........................................... 9.95
FRESH SEA BASS................................................ 9.95
FRESH PETRALE SOLE............................................10.75
FRESH HAWAIIAN AHI............................................10.95
```

FEATURED ITEMS

```
MAINE LOBSTER TAILS, BROILED..................................16.95
TENDER CALAMARI, TEMPURA...................................... 8.25
FRESH CHICKEN PALMILLIA - ORANGE, LEMON, GARLIC.............. 8.95
FRESH CANADIAN KING SALMON, BROILED WITH DILL CAPER SAUCE.. 12.95
```

SAUTEED SEAFOODS
WINE, LEMON, BUTTER AND FRESH GARLIC WHEN APPROPRIATE

```
CALAMARI STEAK ALMONDINE...................................... 9.45
FRESH TROUT ALMONDINE......................................... 8.95
CALAMARI STEAK PICCATA........................................ 9.95
FRESH SOLE DORE'..............................................10.25
```

CHICKEN AND BEEF
MESQUITE WOOD CHARCOAL BROILED

```
HAMBURGER WITH CHEESE......................................... 7.25
FRESH CHICKEN BREAST.......................................... 8.95
TOP SIRLOIN...................................................11.50
NEW YORK STEAK................................................15.75
```

SIDE ORDERS
```
STEAMED PARSLEY POTATOES........ 1.00
COTTAGE CHEESE.................. 1.00
FISHERMAN'S RICE............... 1.00
CHERRY TOMATOES................ 1.00
STEAMED BROCCOLI............... 1.45
```

BEVERAGES
```
BREWED COFFEE, TEA.............. .85
PERRIER........................ 1.50
FRUIT JUICES................... 1.50
SOFT DRINKS.................... .85
MILK........................... 1.00
```

WE SPECIALIZE IN COMPANY PARTIES, BANQUETS, & CATERING. PLEASE INQUIRE AT FRONT DESK.

KNOW YOUR PRICES

Make a list of the most commonly ordered items on your restaurant's menu and their current prices. **Commit this list to memory. (The facing page contains a sample menu).**

Menu Item	Price	Menu Item	Price

SAMPLE MENU ABBREVIATIONS AND/OR CODES

Menu Item	Abbreviation/ Code	Menu Item	Abbreviation/ Code
Chateaubriand	CB	Shrimp Cocktail	SMP
Prime Rib (lg)	LPR	Crab Cocktail	CRB
Prime Rib (sm)	SPR		
Rack of Lamp	LAM	French Onion Soup	FO
Skewered Steak	SK	N.E. Clam Chowder	CC
Filet Mignon	FM		
N.Y. Steak	NY		
		Chef Salad	CHEF
Scampi	SC	Seafood Salad	SEA
Abalone	AB		
Lobster Tail	LOB		
Steak and Lobster	COM		
Veal Oscar	VO		
Hamburger	HB		
Club Sandwich	CLUB		
Patty Melt	PM		

WELLNESS		DRESSINGS	
Rare	R	House	H
Medium	M	Green Goddess	GG
Well Done	W	French	FR
		Thousand Island	1000

ABBREVIATIONS AND CODES

Use this page to help you memorize abbreviations of menu items you will need to know to write an order ticket. If your restaurant uses a computer also write down the computer codes you will need to know to enter the order into the computer.

Menu Item	Abbreviation/Code	Menu Item	Abbreviation/Code

SAMPLE BEVERAGE ABBREVIATIONS AND/OR CODES

COMPUTER CODE

500 BOURBON	592 JOHN COLLINS
501 BRANDY	593 JOHNY WALKER RED
502 GIN	595 KAHLUA
503 RUM	596 KAMIKAZI
504 SCOTCH	598 KING ALPHONSE
505 TEQUILA	601 LONG ISLAND ICETEA
506 VODKA	602 MARGARITA
509 ALEXANDER	603 MAI TAI
510 AMARETTO	604 MANHATTAN
515 B&B	605 MARTINI GIN
517 BACARDI COCKTAIL	606 MARTINI VODKA
518 BAILEY'S	609 MEXICAN COFFEE
520 BANANA DAQUIRI	612 OLD FASHIONED
524 BLACK RUSSIAN	618 PINA COLADA *yes*
526 BLOODY MARY	619 PLANTERS PUNCH
528 BRAVE BULL	622 RAMOS FIZZ
529 BRISTOL CREAM	624 REMY MARTIN
530 BLACK LABEL	625 ROB ROY
532 CAMPARI	628 RUSTY NAIL
533 CANADIAN CLUB	633 SALTY DOG
534 CHAMPAGNE CKTL	634 SCHNAPPS
535 CHERRY BRANDY	635 SCREWDRIVER
536 CHI CHI	636 SEAGRAMS 7
537 CHIVAS REGAL	640 SINGAPORE SLING
539 COOLER	642 SLOE GIN FIZZ
540 COURVOISER	646 SOUTHERN COMFORT
550 DAQUIRI	661 TEQUILA SUNRISE
555 DRAMBUIE	662 TIA MARIA
556 DRY SACK	665 TUACCA
557 DUBONNET	670 VERMOUTH DRY
562 EARLY TIMES	671 VERMOUTH SWEET
567 GALLIANO	673 VODKA COLLINS
568 GIN GIMLET	674 VODKA GIMLET
570 GIN SOUR	676 VODKA SOUR
576 GRAND MARNIER	680 WHISKEY SOUR
577 GRASSHOPPER	683 WHITE RUSSIAN
580 HOT APPLE PIE	684 WILD TURKEY
581 HOT BRANDY	685 ZOMBIE
582 HOT BUTTERED RUM	700 BURGUNDY WINE
583 HOT TODDY	701 CHABLIS WINE
585 INTL STINGER	702 ROSE WINE
586 IRISH COFFEE	703 DOMESTIC BEER
590 J & B	704 IMPORTED BEER

BEVERAGE ABBREVIATIONS AND/OR CODES

*This page will help you memorize those beverages you will be serving. It can also help you learn how to write a beverage order or input one into the computer.

BEERS   Abbreviations/Codes   Prices

WINES   Abbreviations/Codes   Prices

COCKTAILS   Abbreviations/Codes   Prices

OTHER BEVERAGES   Abbreviations/Codes   Prices

*(Use additional paper if required.)

PART II
FOLLOW-UP

By now, you should have memorized your **table numbers** in the dining room; the **major menu items** and their **prices**. You also should know the **abbreviations** and/or **codes** necessary to complete an order.

NOW IS THE TIME TO SCHEDULE ANOTHER REVIEW SESSION WITH YOUR MANAGER/TRAINER.

Let your manager/trainer know that you are prepared to complete a verbal test on material covered in this section.

I. _____ , agree to meet with my supervisor/
      (your name)
trainer to demonstrate my knowledge of restaurant table numbers, major menu items, prices and abbreviations and codes.

_____
                  Signature

I, _____ agree to meet with above named
    (name of trainer)
employee to review the items noted above on _____ , at
                                      date
_____ .
      place

_____
                  Signature

PART III

SELLING AND CUSTOMER RELATION SKILLS

- **SELL YOURSELF**

- **SELL YOUR PRODUCTS**

You never
get a
second
chance
to create
a positive
first
impression.

Harold works hard at being a good food server. But several weeks ago he blew it. In addition to working in the restaurant, Harold's hobby is working on his car. One afternoon Harold was working on his car's engine when the restaurant called to ask if he could come in early. In the rush to get to work, Harold quickly washed up. It wasn't until a customer said something to his manager about dirty fingernails that Harold realized he made a cardinal mistake. Harold still works hard at being a good food server, but now is more conscientious than ever about his grooming.

COMMUNICATING YOUR BEST IMAGE

Like an actor or actress, a restaurant server is always on stage with customers. Creating a good first impression is essential. It is important to understand the connection between how you look to yourself and your attitude. The better your self-image when you contact with a customer, the more positive your attitude will be.

Rate yourself on each of the grooming areas presented below. If you circle a 5, you are saying that no improvement is required. If you circle a 1 or 2, you need considerable improvement. Be honest.

	Perfect	Good	Fair	Weak	Poor
1. Hairstyle, and hair grooming	5	4	3	2	1
2. Personal habits of cleanliness (body)	5	4	3	2	1
3. Personal habits of cleanliness (hands and fingernails)	5	4	3	2	1
4. Jewelry (appropriate to situation)	5	4	3	2	1
5. Neatness (shoes shined, clothes clean, well pressed, etc.)	5	4	3	2	1
6. General grooming: Do you feel your appearance will reflect professionalism?	5	4	3	2	1

WHEN IT COMES TO MY "ON THE JOB" APPEARANCE, I WOULD RATE MYSELF:

EXCELLENT ☐   GOOD ☐   NEED IMPROVEMENT ☐

> MOST SUCCESSFUL RESTAURANT SERVERS
> CLAIM THAT TO BE SHARP MENTALLY YOU MUST
> COMMUNICATE YOUR BEST IMAGE.

SELL YOURSELF
THROUGH YOUR . . .

BODY LANGUAGE

Did you know that body language can account for more than half of the message you communicate?

Here is a body language checklist. Place a check in the square if you can answer "yes" to the question.

☐ Do you hold your head high and steady?

☐ Do your arms move in a natural, unaffected manner?

☐ Are your facial muscles relaxed and under control?

☐ Do you find it easy to maintain a natural smile?

☐ Is your body movement controlled, neither harried nor too casual?

☐ Do you find it easy to maintain eye contact with people you are talking to?

CONSIDER WHY IT IS IMPORTANT TO BE ABLE TO ANSWER "YES" TO THESE QUESTIONS.

BODY LANGUAGE EXERCISE

Four sets of opposite non-verbal messages are presented below.

CAN YOU DESCRIBE THE POSSIBLE MESSAGES THESE FORMS OF BODY LANGUAGE SEND TO CUSTOMERS?

<u>POSITIVE MESSAGES</u>

Face is relaxed and under control.

This communicates _____
_____
_____

Smile is natural and comfortable.

This communicates _____
_____
_____

Eye contact is maintained when talking and listening to others.

This communicates _____
_____
_____

Body movement is relaxed, yet deliberate and controlled.

This communicates _____
_____
_____

<u>NEGATIVE MESSAGES</u>

Face is anxious and uptight.

This communicates _____
_____
_____

Smile is missing or forced.

This communicates _____
_____
_____

Eye contact is avoided when talking and listening.

This communicates _____
_____
_____

Body movement is harried and rushed.

This communicates _____
_____
_____

_____
Compare your comments with those of the author on page 70.

SELL YOURSELF

YOUR TONE OF VOICE

OR

HOW YOU SAY SOMETHING

CAN BE MORE IMPORTANT

THAN THE WORDS

YOU USE!

Kim was a ten-year veteran waitress at a beach-front cafe. The cafe was forced to close temporarily because of a beach redevelopment project. When the cafe reopened as an upscale dinner house Kim was re-hired as a waitress. Kim however, had to learn to make adjustments to the new situation. More than anything, she had to learn to adjust her tone of voice to project a more sophisticated and formal image as required by the new restaurant customer mix.

LISTENING TO THE SOUND OF YOUR OWN VOICE

The tone of voice you use with customers and fellow restaurant employees may—

(1) mean the difference between average tips or **great** tips, and

(2) mean the difference between being an adequate restaurant server and a **great** restaurant server.

Below are voice styles through which restaurant servers communicate. Which one(s) are most like you? Check the one(s) with which you identify the most.

_____ My voice becomes loud and agitated when I am angry.

_____ I tend to speak more quickly when I am nervous.

_____ My voice slows significantly and/or becomes quieter when I get tired.

_____ Others describe my tone of voice as ''upbeat''.

_____ Friends say my tone of voice is warm and understanding when we are in serious conversation.

_____ I can control my tone of voice in most situations.

_____ My voice can sound authoritarian and demanding when required.

_____ Others consider my voice meek.

_____ I'm lucky because my voice is clear, direct and natural.

_____ My vocabulary and style of speaking tends to be serious and scholarly.

Some of these voice styles are more conducive to your success as a restaurant server than others. Please see the author's comments on page 70.

Note: **This may be a difficult exercise for those not accustomed to listening to themselves. If this describes you, ask a friend to help you complete this exercise, it may provide some invaluable insights. Use of a tape recorder or telephone answering device can also be helpful.**

THE EFFECTIVE RESTAURANT SERVER KNOWS THE RIGHT THING TO SAY TO GET THE SALE.

YOU HAVE SET THE STAGE WITH
YOUR POSITIVE FIRST IMPRESSION,
YOUR SMILING BODY LANGUAGE, AND
YOUR FRIENDLY TONE OF VOICE . . .

NOW WHAT SHOULD YOU <u>SAY</u> TO GET THE SALE?

SAYING THE RIGHT THING...TO GET THE SALE

Following are some approaches which can help make a larger or extra sale in your restaurant. After each, write your interpretation of what these sales techniques mean.

1. EXPAND MY CUSTOMER'S AWARENESS OF WHAT'S AVAILABLE.
   This means: _____
   _____
   _____

2. EXPLAIN THE FEATURES OF WHAT I AM OFFERING.
   I think this means: _____
   _____
   _____

3. DESCRIBE THE BENEFITS OF WHAT I AM OFFERING.
   This means: _____
   _____
   _____

4. ASK FOR THE ORDER.
   I believe this means: _____
   _____
   _____

5. COMPLIMENT THE CUSTOMER ON HIS/HER CHOICE.
   To me, this means: _____
   _____
   _____

Compare your responses to the author's interpretations on page 71.

SUGGESTIVE SELLING MEANS MAKING <u>SPECIFIC</u> SUGGESTIONS TO YOUR CUSTOMERS.

AVOID ASKING GENERAL QUESTIONS, SUCH AS:

1. Would you like anything else?

2. Do you want dessert?

3. All finished?

SUGGESTIVE SELLING MEANS...

MAKING <u>HELPFUL</u> SUGGESTIONS TO YOUR CUSTOMERS.

There are many ways to do this. Here are a few "lines" you may want to use. Place a check (✔) in the box beside ones you would feel comfortable saying to your customers.

(The words in parenthesis are only examples.)

☐   Have you tried our . . . (blueberry tort dessert)?

☐   Our . . . (hamburgers) are great!

☐   May I suggest a . . . (bottle of wine with your meal).

☐   Have you thought about . . . (a side order of mushrooms with your entree)?

☐   Can I tell you about . . . (our fresh fish)?

☐   That's also available with . . . (whipped cream).

☐   Our chef's speciality is . . . (scallops St. Jacque).

☐   How about a hot . . . (cup of coffee)?

☐   Are you ready for . . . (an after-dinner drink)?

☐   My favorite dinner is . . . (the teriaki chicken).

☐   Do you know about . . . (our salad selections)?

☐   I think you might enjoy . . . (our potato skins).

☐   Can I interest you in . . . (a terrific appetizer).

WHEN YOU SELL SOMETHING TO YOUR CUSTOMERS THEY MAY NOT BE FAMILIAR WITH . . .

YOU SHOULD BE ABLE TO ANSWER THESE BASIC QUESTIONS

I. What are the product FEATURES?

   • What are its ingredients?

   • How is it made?

   • What does it resemble?

II. What are the BENEFITS to customers if they buy the product?

   • Why should your customers buy it?

   • What's in it for them?

EXPLAINING FEATURES AND BENEFITS TO CUSTOMERS

Now you have a chance to plan how to sell some actual items from your restaurant's menu. Pick four items and briefly write down features and benefits for each. Write the kind of thing you would <u>actually</u> say to a customer.

EXAMPLE: Apple Pie:

Features: __Our apple pies are home-made the old fashioned way, in a deep dish. They are made daily and served hot.__

Benefits: __A great way to top off your meal.__ _____

ITEM #1:

Name

Features: _____

Benefits: _____

ITEM #2:

Name

Features: _____

Benefits: _____

ITEM #3:

Name

Features: _____

Benefits: _____

ITEM #4:

Name

Features: _____

Benefits: _____

PUTTING YOUR SELLING SKILLS ALL TOGETHER

THE FIVE STEPS OF SUGGESTIVE SELLING:

Example:

1. EXPAND YOUR CUSTOMERS' AWARENESS OF WHAT'S AVAILABLE. (Don't assume they will read the menu.)

"Don't forget about our home-made apple pie."

2. EXPLAIN THE FEATURES OF WHAT YOU ARE SELLING. (Use your product knowledge.)

"It's deep dish and baked fresh daily."

3. DESCRIBE THE BENEFITS OF WHAT YOU ARE SELLING. (Show your enthusiasm.)

"It tastes great!"
or
"It's less filling."

4. ASK FOR THE ORDER. (Be polite and tactful.)

"Shall I bring you a piece?"

5. COMPLIMENT THE CUSTOMER ON HIS/HER CHOICE. (Make your customers feel good about their choice whether or not they follow your suggestions.)

"You're going to love it!"

SELLING SKILLS PRACTICE

When practicing your selling skills, it is easier, at first, to sell something you like very much yourself.

Pick your favorite item from your restaurant's menu and write it below.

My favorite menu item is _____.

Now write a script for yourself that you can use to sell your favorite menu item to your next customer.

1. I can expand my customer's awareness of this item by saying:

   _____

   _____

2. I will explain the features of this item by saying:

   _____

   _____

3. I will describe the benefits of this item by saying:

   _____

   _____

4. I will ask for the order this way:

   _____

   _____

5. I will compliment the customer on his/her choice by telling them:

   _____

   _____

For comparison, see the author's script for selling a bottle of wine on page 71.

WHAT DO YOU DO
WHEN . . CUSTOMERS ARE NOT
SATISFIED OR COMPLAIN???

Steps You Should Take
1. Listen carefully to the complaint.
2. Repeat the complaint back to the customer to insure you heard the complaint correctly.
3. Apologize.
4. Acknowledge the customer's feelings (anger, frustration, dissappointment, etc.).
5. Explain the action you will take to correct the problem.
6. Thank the customer for bringing the problem to your attention.

NEVER:

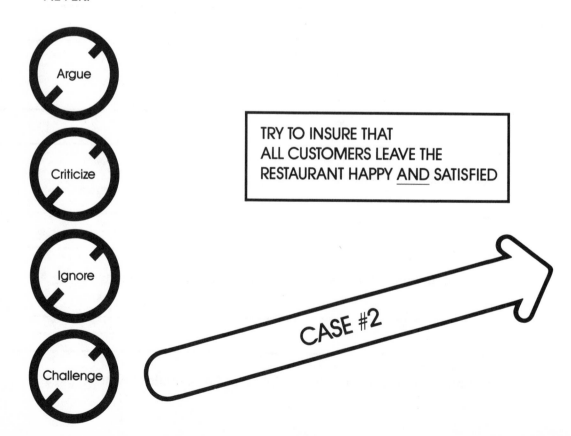

Argue

Criticize

Ignore

Challenge

TRY TO INSURE THAT
ALL CUSTOMERS LEAVE THE
RESTAURANT HAPPY AND SATISFIED

CASE #2

CASE #2
HANDLING CUSTOMER COMPLAINTS

A customer to whom you served a steak dinner a few minutes ago calls you over. He is angry. He informs you that this is the second time he has ordered his steak well done at your restaurant and failed to get it the way he ordered. It is pink in the middle and he wants no pink showing. He accuses you of not taking the order correctly and calls the cooks incompetent. He is making a **big** scene in front of the other customers.

WHAT WILL YOU SAY TO THIS CUSTOMER?

Record your action plan below:

Action

Repeat the complaint: _____

_____

Apologize: _____

Acknowledge feelings _____

_____

Explain what you will do: _____

_____

Thank the customer: _____

_____

See author's comments on page 71.

IT IS TIME TO MEASURE THE PROGRESS
YOU HAVE MADE. ON THE FOLLOW-
ING PAGE ARE 20 STATEMENTS
WHICH ARE EITHER TRUE OR FALSE.
EACH IS WORTH 5 POINTS. ANSWERS
WILL BE FOUND ON PAGE 71.

SUMMARY QUIZ

FINAL EXERCISE:

Mark each question either True or False:

_____ 1. Successful servers constantly need to be the center of attention.

_____ 2. Successful servers view their jobs primarily as selling as opposed to just serving.

_____ 3. Servers have little control over the amount of tips they receive.

_____ 4. As a restaurant server, you are often called upon to apologize to customers for mistakes you did not make.

_____ 5. It really isn't important to remember customers' names and faces.

_____ 6. The procedural side of service is concerned with the systems and procedures used to meet customer needs and wants.

_____ 7. The procedural side of service is more important than the personal side.

_____ 8. Knowing the time requirements for quality service will help you do a better job.

_____ 9. What you do in your section of the restaurant has little effect on the other sections.

_____ 10. Good anticipation means providing items and service to customers without requiring them to ask.

_____ 11. When communicating with another person, it is important to always maintain his or her self-esteem.

_____ 12. Eye contact has little impact on communication.

_____ 13. Customer feedback rarely provides information necessary to do a better job.

_____ 14. The attitude of the server is as important as the quality of food served.

_____ 15. The ability to identify and provide for your customers' needs will enhance the tips you earn.

_____ 16. The life-blood of any restaurant is repeat business.

_____ 17. Your body language often communicates more than the actual words you use.

_____ 18. The best sales people are aggressive.

_____ 19. Knowing the menu thoroughly will help you become a better sales person.

_____ 20. Customer complaints should be encouraged.

ANSWERS ON PAGE 71.

AUTHOR'S NOTES AND COMMENTS

Service Skills Inventory (page 5)
This booklet will help you improve your ability to perform the fourteen behaviors listed. Understanding there is always something more that can be learned about any subject reflects the right frame of mind for proceeding through this book. If you checked, ''know all there is to know'' for any given item, I would like to meet you since I have yet to meet anyone who knows all there is to know about a subject.

Timeliness (page 15)
The value of this exercise is establishing clear expectations between you and your manager/trainer. You may have your own ideas of what is timely, but it is also important to find out what your manager/trainer considers to be timely. In fact, your job may depend upon it.

Anticipate Your Customers' Needs (page 19)

Situation	Anticipated Need
A couple orders one dessert.	An extra spoon, perhaps an extra plate
A customer with a half cup of coffee.	More coffee
A family with two small children.	A high chair or booster chair
You serve a customer a big, gooey, chili-cheese burger.	Extra napkins
A couple is celebrating a birthday.	Possibly champagne, a special dessert or other recognition of the event
Two older customers ordering a single meal.	An extra plate
A customer finished with his meal and looking around.	Coffee and/or his check
A group of four is informed they have a wait before being seated in the dining room.	Beverages and appetizers
Businessmen talking and making notes on a napkin.	A pad or piece of paper
Two people announce they are in a hurry.	Special note to the kitchen to rush the order and recommend a menu item that can be prepared quickly

AUTHOR'S NOTES AND COMMENTS (continued)

Identify the Special Needs of Your Customers (page 31)
<u>AGE</u>

Small children: high chairs, boosters, something to keep them busy (i.e. crackers) extra napkins.

Teenagers: non-alcoholic drinks, lower priced items.

Seniors: less spicy items, smaller portioned items, lower priced items.

<u>DRESS</u>

Casual dress: need to relax and enjoy themselves in an informal way.

Business suit: need to be more formal, perhaps unobtrusive service.

Formal attire: need to attend another engagement or need to celebrate.

<u>GROUP SIZE AND MIX:</u>

Group of ladies: often enjoy fancy drinks and light foods.

After work bunch: often enjoy plenty of drinks and snack foods.

Large family gathering: may need recognition of a special occasion or event.

<u>BODY LANGUAGE:</u>

Arms folded: needs attention, may be angry, waiting or uptight.

Looking around: needs attention; may be looking for you; may need check or something else.

Looking at watch: needs attention; probably in a hurry.

<u>TONE OF VOICE</u>

Uptight: needs to be soothed, shown recognition or made to feel comfortable.

Angry: needs to vent steam at a good listener and empathizer.

Cheerful: needs to be recognized and encouraged.

Provide for the Special Needs of Your Customers (page 33)
Here are at least two ideas (there are more) of how you can provide for the following human needs.

Need to be attended to: Greet them with a warm smile.
Suggest a favorite menu item or two.

Need to feel comfortable and relaxed: Introduce yourself and ask it they are comfortable.
Talk in language that they understand.

Need to belong: Tell them you are glad they are here.
Engage in friendly conversation.

Need to feel important: Do something special for them.
Tune-in to any individual needs.

Need to be recognized: Call them by name.
Recognize that they have been in the restaurant before.

Case #1 The New Food Server (page 37)

How should the manager respond?

The manager must produce an immediate turnaround in Eric's behavior and attitude toward the job since Eric is probably costing the restaurant a great deal of business. The manager does see some potential in Eric, so he should give him one week to turn his attitude and drive around. If no improvement is demonstrated after one week, Eric should be asked to find another job that would be more suitable to his interests.

AUTHOR'S NOTES AND COMMENTS (continued)

Case #1 (Continued)

What does Eric need to do to turn the situation around?

Eric needs to take his job more seriously. He needs to realize there is a great deal to learn about restaurant serving and conscientiously strive to develop these skills as soon as he can. If he can, he should obtain a copy of this book and read it carefully. He also needs to ask his manager for any materials and information about the restaurant and his job that would help him perform better. The next step is for Eric to show that he can actually do the job.

Body Language Exercise (page 53)

Positive Messages:	Negative Messages:
Face is relaxed and under control. This communicates you are prepared, know what you are doing, and/or are comfortable with your role.	Face is anxious and uptight. This communicates you are ill prepared, inexperienced and/or uncomfortable with your role.
Smile is natural and comfortable. This communicates you are sure of yourself, like what you are doing and enjoy your guests.	Smile is forced or phony. This communicates you are unsure of yourself, don't like what you are doing, and/or really don't enjoy your customers.
Eye contact is maintained when talking and listening with guests. This communicates guests are important. Also that you are interested in them, and self-confident.	Eye contact is avoided when talking and listening to customers. Eye contact is avoided when talking and listening to customers. This communicates a lack of interest in customers, and/or you lack the self-confidence to do the job.
Body movement is deliberate and controlled. This communicates you are in control, you are glad to be where you are and that you may be busy that's just part of the job.	Body movement is harried and rushed. This communicates you are not in control of the situation, that you would really like the customers to leave since you are so over burdened.

Listening to the Sound of Your Own Voice (page 55)
The tone of voice that is conducive to your success as a restaurant server can be described by any of these four characteristics:
1. It is upbeat.
2. It is warm, comfortable and understanding.
3. It is under control.
4. It is clear, direct and natural.

AUTHOR'S NOTES AND COMMENTS (continued)

Saying the Right Thing to Get the Sale (page 57).
My interpretation of each of the suggestive selling steps is as follows:
EXPANDING AWARENESS: Let the customer know about any specials or extra items available that may not be on the menu. Outline several options for your customers. Don't assume that they will or want to read the menu.
EXPLAIN FEATURES: This is where your product knowledge comes to good use. Relate how the item is made, what the ingredients are, how it tastes, etc.
DESCRIBE BENEFITS: Here's where your enthusiasm comes in handy. How delicious is the item? Is it a price value? Is the portion generous? What's in it for the customer?
ASK FOR ORDER: Be tactful and polite. Don't be pushy.
COMPLIMENT THE CUSTOMER: Make the customer feel good about his/her choice. Say, "You'll really like it," or "Good choice," or some positive comment to end the interaction on a positive note.

Selling Skills Practice (page 63).
Here is a sample script for selling a bottle of white wine.

"We have a very nice Chenin Blanc on special tonight."

"It is very light and dry," (explaining the features)
"and will go very nicely with your meal." (describing a benefit)

"May I get you a bottle." (asking for the order)

"Very good, I'm sure you will enjoy it." (complimenting the customer's choice)

Handling Customer Complaints (page 65).
A possible dialogue might go something like this"

Server:	"You ordered your steak well done and it came out medium." (repeats the complaint) "I'm really sorry, sir." (apology) "You certainly have a right to be upset. I would be too." (acknowledges feelings) "What I would like to do, if it is okay with you, is take your steak back to the kitchen and have the chef cook it right." (explain action that you will take) "Would that be all right?"
Customer:	"Okay."
Server:	"Thank you for bringing this to my attention. I'm glad you told me about this. This shouldn't be happening." (thanking the customer)

True-False Test (page 67).
1. F (Successful servers make the customer the center of attention.) 2. T 3. F (Servers have a great deal of control over the amount of tips they receive.) 4. T 5. F (Remembering names and faces is one of the most important things you can do as a server.) 6. T. 7. F (They are equally important.) 8. T 9. F (What goes on in each section of the restaurant affects every other section.) 10. T 11. T 12. F (Eye contact has great impact on communication.) 13. F (Customer feedback provides invaluable information to the server.) 14. T 15. T 16 T 17. T 18. F (The best sales people are assertive, and sensitive.) 19. T 20. T

Crisp books are distributed in Canada by Reid Publishing, Ltd., P.O. Box 7267, Oakville, Ontario, Canada L6J 6L6.

In Australia by Prime Learning Australia, Rochedale South, 7 Deputor Street, Brisbane, Queensland.

And in New Zealand by Prime Learning Pacific, 18 Gibbons Road, Weymouth, Auckland.

THE FIFTY-MINUTE SERIES

Quantity	Title	Code #	Price	Amount
	The Fifty-Minute Supervisor—*2nd Edition*	58-0	$6.95	
	Effective Performance Appraisals—*Revised*	11-4	$6.95	
	Successful Negotiation—*Revised*	09-2	$6.95	
	Quality Interviewing—*Revised*	13-0	$6.95	
	Team Building: An Exercise in Leadership—*Revised*	16-5	$6.95	
	Performance Contracts: The Key To Job Success—*Revised*	12-2	$6.95	
	Personal Time Management	22-X	$6.95	
	Effective Presentation Skills	24-6	$6.95	
	Better Business Writing	25-4	$6.95	
	Quality Customer Service	17-3	$6.95	
	Telephone Courtesy & Customer Service	18-1	$6.95	
	Restaurant Server's Guide To Quality Service—*Revised*	08-4	$6.95	
	Sales Training Basics—*Revised*	02-5	$6.95	
	Personal Counseling—*Revised*	14-9	$6.95	
	Balancing Home & Career	10-6	$6.95	
	Mental Fitness: A Guide To Emotional Health	15-7	$6.95	
	Attitude: Your Most Priceless Possession	21-1	$6.95	
	Preventing Job Burnout	23-8	$6.95	
	Successful Self-Management	26-2	$6.95	
	Personal Financial Fitness	20-3	$7.95	
	Job Performance and Chemical Dependency	27-0	$7.95	
	Career Discovery—*Revised*	07-6	$6.95	
	Study Skills Strategies—*Revised*	05-X	$6.95	
	I Got The Job!—*Revised*	59-9	$6.95	
	Effective Meetings Skills	33-5	$7.95	
	The Business of Listening	34-3	$6.95	
	Professional Sales Training	42-4	$7.95	
	Customer Satisfaction: The Other Half of Your Job	57-2	$7.95	
	Managing Disagreement Constructively	41-6	$7.95	
	Professional Excellence for Secretaries	52-1	$6.95	
	Starting A Small Business: A Resource Guide	44-0	$7.95	
	Developing Positive Assertiveness	38-6	$6.95	
	Writing Fitness-Practical Exercises for Better Business Writing	35-1	$7.95	
	An Honest Day's Work: Motivating Employees to Give Their Best	39-4	$6.95	
	Marketing Your Consulting & Professional Services	40-8	$7.95	
	Time Management On The Telephone	53-X	$6.95	
	Training Managers to Train	43-2	$7.95	
	New Employee Orientation	46-7	$6.95	
	The Art of Communicating: Achieving Impact in Business	45-9	$7.95	
	Technical Presentation Skills	55-6	$7.95	
	Plan B: Protecting Your Career from the Winds of Change	48-3	$7.95	
	A Guide To Affirmative Action	54-8	$7.95	
	Memory Skills in Business	56-4	$6.95	

(Continued on next page)

THE FIFTY-MINUTE SERIES
(Continued)

☐ Send volume discount information.

☐ Add my name to CPI's mailing list.

	Amount
Total (from other side)	
Shipping ($1.25 first book, $.50 per title thereafter)	
California Residents add 7% tax	
Total	

Ship to: _____

_____

_____

_____

Phone number: _____

Bill to: _____

_____

_____

_____

P.O. # _____

All orders except those with a P.O.# must be prepaid.
Call (415) 949-4888 for more information.

‖‖‖

BUSINESS REPLY
FIRST CLASS   PERMIT NO. 884   LOS ALTOS, CA

POSTAGE WILL BE PAID BY ADDRESSEE

NO POSTAGE
NECESSARY
IF MAILED
IN THE
UNITED STATES

Crisp Publications, Inc.
95 First Street
Los Altos, CA 94022